Carlos Pascual

GRANADA
AND THE ALHAMBRA

95 Colour illustrations

BONECHI

LA ALHAMBRA

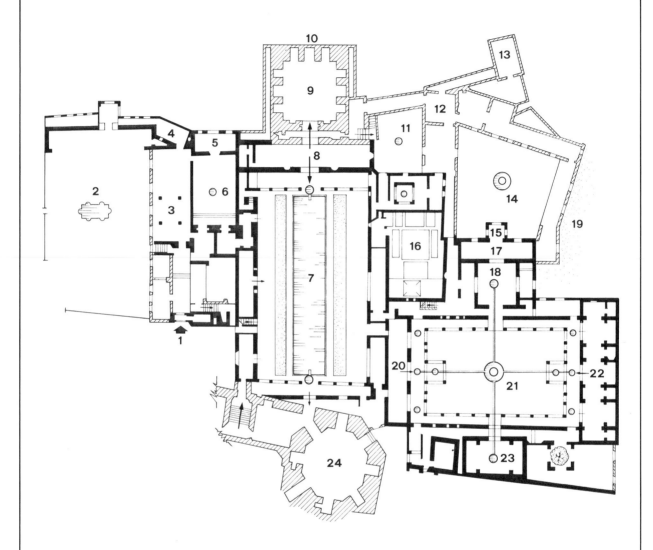

1 - Entrada
2 - Patio de Machuca
3 - Sala del Mexuar
4 - Oratorio del Mexuar
5 - Cuarto Dorado
6 - Patio del Mexuar
7 - Patio de los Arrayanes
8 - Sala de la Barca

9 - Salón de Embajadores
10 - Torre de Comares
11 - Patio de la Reja
12 - Departamentos de Carlos V
13 - Peinador de la Reina
14 - Patio de Lindaraja
15 - Mirador de Lindaraja
16 - Sala de Baños

17 - Sala de los Ajimeces
18 - Sala de las Dos Hermanas
19 - Jardines del Partal
20 - Sala de los Mocárabes
21 - Patio de los Leones
22 - Sala de los Reyes
23 - Sala de los Abencerrajes
24 - Palacio de Carlos V

© Copyright 1996 by CASA EDITRICE BONECHI, Via Cairoli 18/b, Firenze - Italy — Telex 571323 CEB —
All rights reserved. No part of this book may be reproduced without the written permission of the Publisher —
Printed in E.E.C. — *Photographic service by* LUIGI DI GIOVINE - *Translated by* Sonia Ercolini.

Printed in EEC by Centrostampa Bonechi Editore — Firenze-Paris —

The solid mass of the Alhambra is silhouetted against the nearby Sierra mountains.

INTRODUCTION

When the Andalusian poet Manuel Machado tried to describe Granada in only four words, he chose the following: «secret water which cries». The most surprising thing about this Andalusian province, which lies between the highest peaks of the peninsula and the coast, is in fact the proximity of the snow and the sea. It is an amazing fact that in spring the tourists here can ski on the Sierra Nevada slopes in the morning and then lie on the beaches around Motril, Salobreña or Almuñecar in the afternoon. The «secret» water is the soul of Granada as it trickles through the high peaks of the Sierra, feeding its land and re-appearing in abundance in its streams, fountains, and brooks. Granada was the last Arabic redoubt in Spain; at a time when the whole peninsula had been converted back to Christianity, the last Nazarenes accompanied their splendid Baroque architecture with whispering fountains. Granada's soul plays an important role in the architecture of the Naza-rene palaces and homes just like the titles, marble, plaster, interlacing and arabesque decoration. When the last king of Granada was overthrown and defeated by the Catholic Monarchs in 1491, he fled from the city with tears in his eyes: it wasn't caused by a woman's weakness as legend has it but Granada's soul reflecting in his eyes for the last time.

If the Nazarene influence was generous and powerful for Granada, so was the Christian influence. The immense, lengthy shadow of the Alhambra can't hide the string of towers, convents, palaces and hospitals. The existence of so many different cultural elements has created an open and tolerant yet agonizing Unamuno character in the people of Granada; it is no coincidence that Mariana de Pineda, one of the greatest Spanish women myths, and the liberal tormented Ganivet who committed suicide from Granada, nor that Federico García Lorca was shot in Granada, his home-town.

A general view of the Alhambra complex.

The Door of Justice near the Renaissance fountain called Charles V's Basin. ▶

LA ALHAMBRA

On top of a steep hill overlooking the city, the Alhambra rises up, facing its sister hill of Albaicín, separated from it by the Darro river, with the snow-tipped peaks of the Sierra Nevada in the background. Known as the Bermejo Castle, which comes from the Arabic word alluding to the red clay used to build its walls, it is the oldest, most impressive and best preserved Arabic palace in the world.

The first Nazarene king, Alhamar, decided to move his court from Albaicín, the main settlement, to the next neighbouring hill in 1238. Alhamar's successors continued to expand the monumental structure. Abu Hachach Yusuf I and his son and heir, Mohamed V, were the instigators of the main transformation and construction in the XIV century, which still exists today. The complex of towers, walls, palaces and gardens was adapted to the land's structure and was inspired by the finest oriental spirit. After the Christian

A view of the Alcazaba, the earliest portion of the Alhambra, and its strong towers.

◄ *The Puerta del Vino, or Wine Gate.*

conquest in the XV century, it continued to be the royal palace and underwent new constructions and transformations.

After the first ritual ascent of the Cuesta de Gomérez walking through the romantic avenues with their downward flow of fresh, sparkling water, we finally come face to face with one of the richest and most complete monumental complexes. We can begin this visit at the last of Granada's doors (XVI century); on the right the Bermejas towers, erected in the XI or XII century to reinforce the wall, loom up. After crossing the avenue, which can be done by car, we have to go through the Puerta de la Justicia and then through the Puerta del Vino to reach the spacious Plaza de los Algibes; it owes its name to the underground deposits laid down in the XVI century and can be used as a reference point to visit different sectors.

In chronological order, we can begin our visit at the *Alcazaba* which is, as its name indicates, a castle to

defend the residential palaces of the Alhambra. Between it and the Alcazaba you will pass through the Adarve garden, a simple garden filled with the scent of boxwood, used in the past as a defense weapon. The most important part of the Alcazaba is the *Torre de la Vela*, thus named as it watched over the city from its strategic position; there the alarm was sounded in times of danger and its bell regulated the irrigation shift.

From the tower we can enjoy and appreciate this unequalled view. In the distance we can see the snow-tipped peaks of the Sierra and down below the new city spreading out towards the Vega round about the palaces and gardens. In the middle of the Alcazaba we find the Plaza de Armas where we can observe the remains of small military quarters. The Puerta and Torre de Armas overlooks the Albaicín.

After the preliminary visit we can now enter into the intimate world of the residential palaces, where delicate details and refined sensuality contrast with the harsh military enclosure and weapons. Fundamentally, the palace is built around two patios — the Patio de los Arrayanes and the Patio de los Leones. Around the Patio de los Arrayanes all public activities such as public

audiences, meeting and receptions took place. The rooms around the Patio de los Leones where the sultan's private life envolved, have a more intimate and familiar character.

Leaving the Machuca gardens on your left you enter the *Sala del Mexuar* or Sala del Consejo, which underwent the greatest change when Charles V converted it into an oratory in 1629. Nevertheless remains of the original colours of the ornamental tiles and the arabesque plaster decoration from the times of Mohamed V are still preserved; the interlacing designs of the small chapel at the end of the room have recently been restored. With regard to these renovations, it would be useful to consult Gallego Burín's observations in his classical *Artistic and historical guide to the city of Granada*: «despite the present homogeneity of these structures, there are however some essential differences between the later palaces. While on one hand the Comares is essentially Muslim, the Leones is characterized by Christian variations and influences, which undoubtedly originate from the relationship between the architect, Mohamed V, and the king of the Castle, Peter I. It's sometimes difficult to explain these differences due to

The main hall of the Mexuar, transformed
during the XVIIth century into a Christian chapel.

The north door of the Mexuar's Patio.

◄ The Torre de la Vela offering
one of the most scenic views
from the Alhambra.

◄ *The magnificent ceiling of the Cuarto Dorado in worked, gilded wood.*

The Patio of the Myrtles, with the 45 metre high tower of Comares, the Alhambra's highest construction.

chronological problems with regard to the Alhambra caused by frequent renovations and numerous restorations carried out since the Catholic Monarchs' reign, first by Mouresque architects whose work was easily confused with past works and later perfected in modern times».

After crossing the Patio del Mexuar, with its marble paving, we arrive at the *Cuarto Dorado*, also called Cuarto del Mexuar, de la Mezquita, and de Comares (the toponymy of the whole Alhambra varies according to guides and causes a great deal of confusion).

The south façade is the most impressive part of the Cuarto Dorado and proves to be one of the most interesting elements in the whole Alhambra with its best Nazarene stuccoes and ornamental tiles.

Finally we come out onto the famous Patio de Comares, best known as the Patio de los Arrayanes or de los Mirtos (*arrayán* is the Arabic equivalent of the Greek-Latin term *myrtle*) or de la Alberca or del Estanque... The **Patio de los Arrayanes** which looks bigger than it really is (36.5 m by 23.5 m) sums up all the equilibrium and serenity of Nazarene architecture even though it has undergone many architectural changes (the rooms in the south gallery were destroyed to fit in the Renais-

sance Machuca palace). In the XIX century, a family of architects, José, Rafael and Mariano Contreras carried out so many alterations that rumour has it that the Contreras family were the authentic builders of the Alhambra! Fortunately the last conservationists and restorers erased all traces of these alterations and tried to bring the rooms back to their original form.

The patio is dominated by the powerless presence of the **Torre de Comares** which is part of the walled enclosure. It is sombre and threatening with its embrasures, battlements and huge structure, emphasizing the public and official nature of this section. An elegant door delicately reflected in the surface of the pool gives access to the **Sala de la Barca** which is not named after the keel shape cedar panelling but derives from the Arabic word *baraka* meaning blessing or look. The room's ceiling burnt down in a fire in 1890 and had to be completely rebuilt. It was used as the anteroom for the **Salon de Embajadores**, the biggest in the palace; it served as a throne room where the Sultan received foreign emissaries. This square-shaped room is more than eleven metres long and almost twenty metres high. Each side of the room looks out onto three balconies; there is a twin centre balcony, and above it, windows with wooden

11

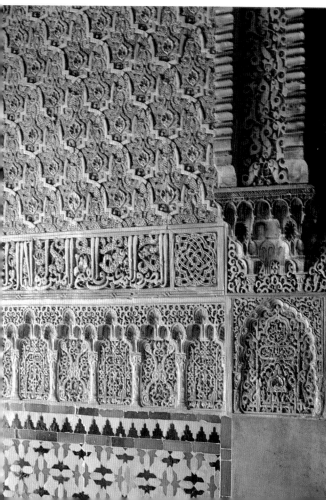

*Four images of the Ambassadors'
Room lavishly decorated with
marble and glazed tiles.
Below, to the right,
the Torre del Peinador.*

13

In these pages, three views of the
celebrated Lions' Patio, which
has become the Alhambra's symbol.

On the next two pages, yet another ▶
two details of the Lions' Patio.

shutters dominated by linear and graphic forms let the
light filter through.

From these balconies we can enjoy the best view over
the avenue which goes down towards the Darro River.
The decoration is a prodigy of finely entwining strands
of plasterwork which has a hypnotic effect on whoever
looks at it. According to tradition, the signing of the
surrender pact of the city by the Moorish King Boadbil
El Chico to the Catholic Monarchs took place in this
room. Another legend affirms that Queen Isabel offered
her jewels to Columbus here to finance his journey to
the unknown. Not to mention other stories and legends
about Boabdil and his mother...

Returning to the Patio de los Arrayanes, in front of us
stands another twin door which is reflected on the opposite side of the pool. The room above is said to have
housed the Monarch's *harem*.

On the opposite side of the Patio de los Arrayanes,
there is a small slope which leads us into the most intimate and private sector of the palace. The **Patio de los
Leones** is a magnificent man-made oasis which opens
out into different rooms. The fine white marble columns spread out like graceful palm trees and lead to-

Yet three pictures of
the Lions' Patio decoration.

*Two views of the Sala de los Abencerrajes
and, to the right, the arch in
the Sala de los Reyes.*

wards the centre fountain filled with sparkling water which reflects the light and illuminates the dark rooms. There are 124 columns, some in groups of two, three or four as in the pavillions. Despite their elegant and stylish similarity, they are in fact all different. The pavillions' interlacing patterns are a splendid example of carpentry and with the columns give rise to a palm-tree, oasis effect, perhaps the only prevailing image in one of the smallest yet best-known patios in the world (28×15 metres, only 441 square metres).

The twelve archaic, stylized lions which carry a cup on their backs, are of more recent (XVI century) but the cup itself is a splendid piece dating back to centuries before. On the brim, there is a part of the *inscription* dedicated by the poet Zemreo to Mohamed V engraved in the marble; amongst other things it asks: «Is it by chance that this garden offers us a work whose beauty is to remain unique in the eyes of God?». The fountain's primitive appearance has been covered up, like the oriental pavillion, since a second cup was added to the

fountain in the XVII century, and a third one in 1838, and the pavillion was covered with a strange dome. Coming out of the harem, after intruding on the Sultan's private quarters, we find on the west-side the **Sala de los Mocárabes**, named after the work on its ceiling, although it was destroyed in an explosion in 1590 and rebuilt in the XVII century (today we can see part of the early and new section). A patio opens up through three archways.

On the right side, the **Sala de los Abencerrajes** broods in its sombre memories: according to a dubious legend, the monarch, uncertain whether it was Mohamed, Muley, Hacen, or Boabdil, ordered the beheading of the famous high class nobles of the Abencerrajes; according to tradition, the rusty-red marks on the marble of the fountain were caused by the blood of the defeated warriors who were sacrificed one by one as they entered the room.

On the side opposite the Sala de los Mocárabes: the **Sala de los Reyes** or Sala del Tribunal, or de la Justicia.

It is divided into sections corresponding to the three arches at the entrance forming dome-covered sections with arch windows at the starting-points.

At the end of the room, bedrooms open up to us containing the most curious decorations of the whole section: leather paintings which line the wooden dome. They are not top quality but are interesting because of the lack of representational art in the whole Alhambra enclosure. According to Gallego Burín «much has been said about these paintings which are undoubtebly Christian». In fact, they date back to the XIV century and were probably painted by Christian artists from Seville: some critics dare to say that the artist was of Tuscan origin or training due to the Italian style of these oil paintings of sultans and their ancestors.

Finally, on the other side, we come to one of the most beautiful Baroque rooms in the Alhambra, the **Sala de**

The dome with stalactites ▶
in the Sala de las Hermanas.

The beautiful perspective
of the Sala de los Reyes or Hall
of Justice.

One of the frescoes that decorate
the ceiling of the Sala de los Reyes
with the dazzling colours
of a Persian miniature.

*A detail of the decoration of the
Sala de las dos Hermanas, one of the
palace's most sumptuous rooms.*

*One of the twin balconies ▶
in the Sala de los Ajimeces.*

The exquisite Mirador de Daraxa (or Lindaraja)
with its beautiful stuccowork
on the walls similar to inlaid ivory.

The small, poetic Lindaraja Garden
seen from above.

las dos Hermanas, named after the two great white
marble sister flagstones in the middle of the room acting
as a background for the indoor fountain. The rooms
seemingly formed the living quarters of the sultan and
his family, and here his sons' official brides were
confined if renounced by the monarchy. The tiled panelling, the colours of the plaster, and the dome's interlacing turn this room into a rich, extravagant jewel. The
room, built during the last days of the reign of Mohamed V, reveals two small rooms at the side, one called
the **Sala de los Ajimeces**, thus named because of the
twin balconies which look onto the garden (they aren't
exactly «ajimeces» because the ajimez is a raised, enclosed balcony with shutters), is covered with a precious roof probably built in a later period (XVI century).

The **Mirador de Daraja** or Daraxa is named after the
Arab expression «i'ain dar aixa» which means «the eyes
of the sultan's house»; however according to one of the
many legends about the palace, the name comes from
Lindaraja, the daughter of the governor of Malaga for
whom this extravagant romantic fantasy was supposed-
ly built.

It is even more beautiful if we remember that it was
built with plain and simple materials like plaster, tiles,

*The multicoloured decoration
of the Hammam, or bathroom.*

ceramic... and also with elements like light, shadows, water, landscape and above all with imagination. On the walls is an inscription contemplating the immense beauty: «I have brought together such beauty that the stars in the heavenly skys are lit up by it»; in another line which maybe alludes to the magic of some of the ephemeral elements: «when one contemplates my beauty he is deluded with outward appearance».

At the intersection of the two main sections of the Alhambra, the Comares palace and El Cuarto de los Leones, we discover the *Hamman* or **Sala de Baños**, on a different level. To reach them go down the Patio de la Reja or de los Cipreses, after crossing Charles V's rooms.

The rooms were built at the time when the emperor intended to make Granada the capital of his kingdom, but he never used them. On the other hand, the North American writer, Washington Irving, used four of these rooms as a setting for his romantic «Tales of the Alhambra» in 1829. In 1959 to commemorate his centenary, some of the romantic scenes were acted out here. The rooms were built over the garden and on the «Torre de Abul Hachach» wall converting it and its tower to the **Galeria del Tocador** and **Tocador de la Reina** for the

An overview of the white houses
of the Albaicín from one of
the numerous miradores.

The "resting room" in the royal bathrooms, ▶
with four columns supporting the central
part and a fine decoration of majolicas forming
a mosaic in the niches which open on the walls.

empress Isabel, Charles V's ill-fated wife. The Peinador and Gallery are in fact two good balconies which decorate the tower, painted by two of Raphael's disciples, Julio Aquiles and Alejandro Mayner.

The baths which date back to the time of Yusuf, underwent some dubious «restorations» in the XIX century (carried out by Contreras). We first enter the Sala de las Camas from where the king could look at the women coming out of the baths and then throw an apple to the one he desired.

The actual bath room quarters feature simple architecture, only decorated with ornamental tiles and which ironically have suffered little changes.

The **Jardín de Lindaraja**, or de Daraxa or de los Narajos or de los Mármoles, is connected to the baths. It was built by Charles V's architects and was made to replace a terrace or garden at the far end of the Mirador de las dos Hermanas. A Mouresque fountain prevails in this dark and silent corner; its basin was brought here from Mexuar and placed on top of a wooden shaft inside another Renaissance basin. On the brim of the basin we can read the poem written in the memory of Ben Nasar: «I am a great ocean with elegant marble shores and my pearly-white sea spreads out over a finely engraved surface».

From the Jardín de Lindaraja we can begin an interesting tour of the walls and towers which enclose the palace up to the Puerta de la Justicia from where we entered. First of all we cross the **Jardínes del Partal** built in a later period, over the military and servants' quarters

In these four pictures, the Gardens of the Partal, ▶
with its five arches thate are reflected
in the quiet waters of the basin. The inlaid wooden
ceiling inside the Partal is worth looking at.

and its gardens. We find the Torre de las Damas, which seems to rest beside a peaceful pool, that reveals a richly carved gateway, *partal* meaning gateway. The lions which stand guard on the edge of the pool were brought here in 1843 when the asylum was demolished; it is an institution which proves how the Moslems in Granada were more civilised and rational than the Christians in the rest of Spain, who still believed madness to be an act of the devil. Behind the palm trees reflected in the pool stand three dwelling quarters of the Yusuf period; one of them houses some of the most interesting Mouresque paintings which were discovered in 1907 and prove to be unique in Muslem Spain. These paintings contradict the harsh theory that the Koran clearly prohibited the paintings of live human beings. The hunting scenes and fantastic animals, alongside musicians, singers and warriors are closely related to the Persian manuscripts of the XIII century. Further on, beside the Torre del Mihrab, there is a small mosque of the Yusuf I period which defends the Puerta de Hierro, the Torre del Cadí and the Torre de la Cautiva, decorated during the Yusuf period and where, according to legend, Lady Isabel de Solís, the favourite Christian character of Muley Halen, was kept prisoner: there is an important inscription in the plaster «stop and observe how each figure delicately follows the next». The Torre de las Infantas follows, in memory of the legendary Zaida, Zoraida and Zorahaida created by Washington Irving, already showing signs of the decadence of Nazarene art.

It is important to remember that even after the Christian conquest the Alhambra was still used as the royal palace. Therefore the presence of the Christian monarchs can still be felt in this great monument.

*The dome of the Torre de la
Cautiva seen from below.*

THE PALACE OF CHARLES V

Pedro Machuca began building the palace in 1526 in an Italian Renaissance style popular at the time. After his death in 1550, his son Luis continued his work until it was discontinued in the XVII century leaving the palace incomplete; General Franco then ordered the completion of the palace.

It is an atypical structure built according to Spanish tradition, and it emphasizes the strong Italian influence of the time. «It is one of the noblest architectural creations of the Renaissance period and may be one of the most beautiful examples outside Italy», according to Gallego Burín. Despite popular opinion, Machuca did not destroy any Arab structures but made use of the Moslem *randa* or royal cemetary. It rests on doric columns downstairs and ionic columns above. Passing through the Plaza de los Aljibes and the Puerta de la Justicia, we come across two beautiful doorways: the first one is decorated with reliefs by Juan de Orea and Antonio de Leval in the lower part and Juan de Misares in the upper part, and the second one with sculptures by Nicolao de

The solid façade of Charles V's palace and the vast circular courtyard inside it, with the doric columns of the lower open gallery and the ionic columns of the upper one.

*An overview of the circular courtyard
of Charles V's palace featuring
a double level of galleries with columns.*

Corte. In the nearest corner to the Patio de los Arrayanes stands an octagonal chapel left incomplete because of the projecting dome.

The palace holds the *Museo de Arte Hispanomusulman* and the *Museo de Bellas Artes*. The first contains a collection of capitals, arabesque plasterwork, wooden carvings, ceramics and various relics found during the excavations carried out in the Alhambra. One of the most outstanding pieces is the *«Alhambra vase»* one of the best and rarest examples of Hispanoarabic ceramics of the XIV century, decorated and engraved in blue and gold on a white background.

The Museo de Bellas Artes houses a rich collection of impressive paintings and sculptures by local artists.

Two of the most outstanding artists come from the school of Granada. Juan Sanchez Cotán (1560-1627), originally from the province of Toledo, became Carthusian in 1603 and lived in the Carthusian monastery in Granada until his death, painting pictures for the refectory and cells of the monastery. His strange darkness must have inspired Zurbarán, who shares the honour of being one of the most talented still-life artists in Spain, a simple, plain style which contrasts with the exuberant

The magnificent sculpture to be found ad the entry to the Fine Arts Museum.

A partial view of the hall dedicated to the artist Pedro Anastasio Bocanegra, with the story of the Virgin Mary.

The hall of the Italian fireplace, with
the XVIth century fireplace
in the wall in the background.

A partial view of the hall dedicated to the artist Sanchez ▶
Cotán, and the hall dedicated to Alonso Cano, XVIIth century
artist and leading representative of the Granada school.

and free still-life which was popular at the time in Italian and Flemish art.

Another great artist from Granada is Alonso Cano (1601-1667) who occupies an entire room in the museum.

He was an architect, painter and sculptor who worked in Seville and in the Madrid court, appointed by the Conde-Duque de Olivares. After losing his second wife, who was assassinated under mysterious circumstances in 1664, he retired to the Carthusian monastery in Valencia of Porta Coeli and ended his days in solitude and poverty. His strong character is personified in his works, and while his dark paintings were highly praised by his contemporaries, he went against the popular and affluent Italian and Flemish styles.

There are also some good examples of the work of other Spanish artists and sculptors, for example, Roberto Alemán, Iacopo L'Indaco, Diego de Siloé, Juan de Maeda, Juan de Orea and Vicente Carducho, an Italian emigrant in Spain and a follower of Sanchez Cotán; Pedro de Moya, who has a room dedicated to him, paints with a subtle sensitivity and was influenced by Alonso Cano. Pedro de Mena is also represented with four great paintings which he completed in collaboration with Cano, which we can see in a room dedicated to him. In the **Salón de la Chimenea Italiana**, named after the multicoloured marble XVI century fireplace which was bought in Genoa in 1546 to decorate the palace, XVI and XVII century paintings, tapestries, pieces of furniture and armour are exhibited.

JARDINES DEL GENERALIFE

These gardens dominate the Alhambra complex; the word 'generalife' means either 'raised garden or divine garden' or 'garden of the architect *Genna-Alarif*. The gardens were used at recreation times by the Nazarene royal family. From the simple architectural structures we can enjoy an extensive view of the city and La Vega with the Alhambra in the foureground. We are not interested in the architecture but mainly in the gardens themselves which embrace the delicate and sensitive style described by a famous Andalusian composer, Manuel de Falla, in his «Nights in the Spanish gardens». Every summer, sessions of the classic International Music and Dance Festival are performed on this splendid, natural stage surrounded by cypress trees.

Three pictures of the Generalife Gardens, with the narrow canal flanked by jets of water, rose-bushes, orange trees and cypresses: an oasis of quiet, peace and silence.

An overview of the massive
structure of the Cathedral.

The Cathedral's façade, which Alonso Cano ▶
erected partially changing the
original project by Diego de Siloè.

A view of the Cathedral's apse. ▶

The Door of Pardon, with ▶
its rich Baroque decoration

THE CATHEDRAL

The Christian conquest of the Arabs affected the spirit at the time in the same way as the contemporary adventure of the discovery of new lands. Therefore we can understand why the Catholic Monarchs, who had completed the historical unification and laid down the foundation of a modern state now open to the discovery of a new world, symbolically chose Granada as their base.

Following their example, families and Christian institutions filled Granada with splendid monuments which are only surpassed by the presence of the Alhambra.

The most famous Christian nucleus is clearly the Cathedral with the Royal Chapel used as the Monarchs' mausoleum, the Sagrario, the Lonja de Mercaderes and other buildings like the Palacio Arzobispal, the Palacio de la Madraza or Cabildo Antiguo etc. Enrique de Egas

◀ *A view of the Cathedral's sumptuous interior, which appears to be completely dominated by the contrast between the gold of its decoration and the white of its architecture.*

Front view of the Gate of Pardon. In the following pages, the cathedral's interior.

began building the cathedral in a Gothic style in 1523 but Diego de Siloé continued his work in a Renaissance style with five spacious naves. It was consecrated in 1561 but the work continued until 1703. The façade was designed by Alonso Cano and enriched with reliefs by J. Risueño and L. Verdiguier in the XVIII century. The most outstanding doors are the San Jerónimo door by Siloé and that of the ecclesiastic school which features bas-reliefs also by Siloé.

The **Capilla Mayor** is the most beatiful chapel in Spain with statues by Alonso de Mena of the *apostles* and *statues of the Catholic Monarchs praying* by Pedro de Mena as well as paintings by Juan de Sevilla, Bocanegra, and Alonso Cano. The stained-glass windows on the dome are attributed to Juan del Campo according to a Siloé design. The organs are XVIII century and the altar paintings are by Juan de Sevilla and Bocanegra. There are many pieces in the cathedral and its chapels which are worth pointing out, thanks to famous artists like Alonso Cano, Ribera, Martinel Montañes... although the most precious jewel is still the Capilla Real.

Built in a flowery Gothic style by Enrique de Egas between 1505 and 1507 to house the remains of the Catholic Monarchs, who were buried there in 1521, the

The external access to the Gothic Royal Chapel,
which houses the mortal remains
of Ferdinand and Isabelle.

On the next two pages: the plateresque retablo
on the high altar, the ornate statues
of the two Catholic Kings and, under the crypt,
the simple royal sarcophagi.

◄ The Capilla Dorada inside the cathedral.

Behind the magnificent wrought-iron grates,
the mausoleum of the Catholic Monarchs Ferdinand
and Isabelle, sculptured by the Florentine
Domenico Fancelli in Carrara marble. Alongside
are the tombs of Philip the Handsome
and Joan the Mad by B. Ordóñez.

The interior of the Sacresty, ▶
a real museum of Flemish painting.

Maestro de la Sangre: Pietà. ▶

Capilla Real is enclosed by a railing which is a splendid piece of craftmanship, by Bartolomé de Jaén (1518). *The Monarchs' Tomb* in Carrara Marble is a work of art by Domenico Fancelli. Later the remains of the monarch's daughter, Juana de la Loca, and her unfortunate husband Felipe el Hermoso were brought there and laid in a tomb by Bartolomé Ordoñēz (1526). Iacopo l'Indaco's altarpiece dominates the high altar with sculptures by Felipe de Borgoña and reliefs describing the conquest of Granada and the mass conversion of the Moors. In the transept is to be found the *altar's shrine* by Alonso de Mena (1632). On the left, we can admire an outstanding piece by Dierik Bouts, a colourful *trip-*

tych with figurines constituting one of his best works of art. Below, in the crypt, lie lead sarcophagi which were ransacked and emptied during the war against Napoleon's soldiers.

The Royal Chapel's **Sacristy** was built in elegant Renaissance style between 1705 and 1750. Of its contents, the Renaissance font by Francesco l'Indaco is worth pointing out.

The **Lonja de Mercaderes** beside the Royal Chapel is silver-plated and was built in 1518 by Juan Garcia de Prades. In the Palacio de la Madraza, once an old Arab university (its name is a derivation of «Medersa»), Granada's first town council was set up.

LA ALCAICERIA

Next to the Palacio Arzobispal and in front of the Plaza de Bibarrambla, the Alcaiceria, sprawls an ancient Arab silk bazaar, now invaded by tourism. It is an example of how the Moorish spirit lived on in this Christian nucleus. The same reigning spirit is felt in the Corral del Carbón, and in the nearby streets and is the only example of *fondouk* or Arab inn in Europe.

The Triptych of Passion,
one of Dirk Bout's masterpieces.

The characteristic bazaar of the Alcaicería,
rebuilt in Moorish style
at the end of the last century.

A WALK AROUND GRANADA

The Moslem Alhambra and Christian Cathedral have not exhausted the monumental wealth of the city. It is necessary to organize some walks to discover other monuments which are only excelled by the omnipres-ence of the two main structures.

The first walk takes us to the **University**, founded in 1526 and later set up in a XVIII century Jesuit school. Next to the university, we can admire the Renaissance church of S. Justo and Pastor and the Colegio Mayor of S. Bartholomé and Santiago, both dating back to the XVI century. But the most interesting part of this walk are two nearby churches: the Iglesia de S. Jerónimo by Siloé which houses the tomb of Gonzalo de Córdoba, the Great Captain, with two Renaissance and Gothic patios and the Iglesia de S. Juan de Dios, one of the best Baroque architectural archievements in Granada with its facade decorated with bas-reliefs and statues. Next to it, the **Hospital de S. Juan de Dios** features a monumental staircase in one of its courtyards.

St. Jerome's church.

The façade of St. Jerome and the multi-coloured, sculptured Renaissance retablo.

The staircase in the Hospital ▶
of San Juan de Dios.

The large façade with towers
of the basilica of San Juan de Dios.
Below, a view of the magnificent interior.

The square dedicated
to Catholic Queen Isabella
with the monument
featuring the sovereign.

◀ The Plaza Nueva
and the fountain
of Puerta Real.

The simple, plain façade
of the Carthusian monastery.

The "Coro de legos" inside the Carthusian
monastery, with paintings
by Sanchez Cotán.

The sumptuous, rich decoration of the sacresty, ▶
attributed to Luis de Arévalo.

LA CARTUJA

From St. Cristopher's viewpoint, we can walk to another interesting monument, la Cartuja, now known as the «Baroque Alhambra». Founded by Fernando Gonzalo de Cordoba in 1516, it only consists of the church, the sacristy, and cloister with some annexes. After walking through the silver doorway and past a great staircase we reach a type of hallway where we find the first paintings by Sanchez Cotán who, as already mentioned, was a Carthusian monk; we then visit the extravagantly decorated choir and choir stalls. The presbytery, dominated by an Assumption under a canopy, lies opposite it. The nave is surrounded by a series of Bocanegra paintings including the «Conception» at first thought to be painted by Alonso Cano, and another four paintings

by Sanchez Cotán filled with an aura of mystic symplicity which was characteristic of this monk-artist. From behind the altar we enter the **Holy Sanctuary**, a small lavish Baroque room built by Francisco Hurtado Izquierdo in the first quarter of the XVIII century.

The tabernacle is formed by a canopy resting on columns covering the pavillon and is used as a sanctuary. The sculptures are by José Risueño and Duque Cornejo. The same frenetic style of the columns prevails in this section. We can feel this movement in the frescoes by Palomino and Reina in the copper dome like the angels wings and saints vestments stirred by the breath of the Holy Spirit.

The church and sanctuary's lavish decorations are ex-

The splendid high altar with its canopy inside the Carthusian monastery.

The refectory, with the stories of St. Bruno of Cotán, in one of the few remaining parts of the old XVIth century monastery.

celled by Arévalo and Cabello's baroque **Sacristy**, to which we gain access through a door on the right. Here the columns, panels, capitals, domes and even the floor are overcome by the same frenzy. The Moresque geometric and linear architecture of the Alhambra is in direct contrast with the disordered and disruptive Baroque style.

As Pemán beatifully writes: «We are standing before a symphony of Lamjarón marble, carved stone, mirrors, cream plaster, silver inlays, ivory, ebony, etc. forming an architectural earthquake».

It is not difficult, on the other hand, to think of the relationship of this vivid scene with the Creole-Christian ornaments in South American churches. In comparison, in the refectory besides the cloister, we come across the stark simplicity of the Gothic domes depicting the simple scenes of St. Bruno's life by Sanchez Cotán. The painting of the Carthusian order's holy founder which for a long time was attributed to Alonso Cano, is in fact by Mora and according to a well-known joke among the guides, if you remain silent it's because you're Carthusian...

Two views of the neighborhood of Albaicín.

In the Albaicín district the Arab Baths are still standing, with their Roman and Visigothic capitals dating back to the XIth century.

The district of Albaicín. ▶
In the "cuevas" of the Albaicín, the characteristic caves dug into the face of the mountain, one can attend one of the typical dances of the Spanish gypsies who still live in the district. The cueva Zambra de la Rojo, one of the most famous ones.

ALBAICIN

Another palace to visit at all costs is the sister hill of the Alhambra, the Albaicín, which was the first Moorish colony set up by the Moors who came from Baeza; the name *Rabad al Baecin* comes from here. After the Christian conquest, the Moors united in this redoubt until the Christmas revolt in 1568 when many were massacred and the majority were expelled.

However the Moresque influence prevails over this area. Walking along the steep streets, we come across small squares, patios filled with flowers, Moorish houses and important churches and monuments. The *Iglesia de San Nicolas* is worth visiting as you can enjoy a splendid view of the Alhambra. So is the *Iglesia de San Sal-*vador, a Mudejar church erected on the site of an ancient mosque. From the *Iglesia de San Cristóbal* we can enjoy an interesting view over the Alcazaba Cadima and its enclosure, built in the XI century on the remains of a Visigothic wall.

The Bañuelo, **Arab baths**, attract many tourists; although they are in a bad state of repair, they are still worth visiting just to see their Visigothic and Roman columns, beside the Moresque ones. «The baths seemingly date back to the XI century and are the most important example of Arab public baths in Spain and the oldest works in Moslem Granada», states Gallego Burín.

INDEX